Images of War
Operation Barbarossa

Hitler's Invasion of Russia

Hans Seidler

Edited By Ian Baxter

Pen & Sword
MILITARY

First published in Great Britain in 2010 by
PEN & SWORD MILITARY
an imprint of
Pen & Sword Books Ltd,
47 Church Street,
Barnsley,
South Yorkshire.
S70 2AS

Copyright © Hans Seidler, 2010

A CIP record for this book is available from the British Library.

ISBN 978 1 84884 329 5

The right of Hans Seidler to be identified as author of this work has been asserted by him in accordance with the Copyright, Designs and Patents Act 1988.

All rights reserved. No part of this book may be reproduced or transmitted in any form or by any means, electronic or mechanical including photocopying, recording or by any information storage and retrieval system, without permission from the Publisher in writing.

Printed and bound by CPI UK

Pen & Sword Books Ltd incorporates the imprints of
Pen & Sword Aviation, Pen & Sword Maritime, Pen & Sword Military,
Wharncliffe Local History, Pen & Sword Select, Pen & Sword Military Classics,
Leo Cooper, Remember When, Seaforth Publishing and Frontline Publishing

For a complete list of Pen & Sword titles please contact
Pen & Sword Books Limited
47 Church Street, Barnsley, South Yorkshire, S70 2AS, England
E-mail: enquiries@pen-and-sword.co.uk
Website: www.pen-and-sword.co.uk

Contents

Introduction 5

Chapter One
Invasion Unleashed 7

Chapter Two
Summer Battles 49

Chapter Three
Operation Typhoon 94

Chapter Four
Winter Warfare 127

German Order of Battle 167
Soviet Order of Battle 171

Introduction

Barbarossa was the code-name for the invasion of the Soviet Union by Nazi Germany. It was the largest military invasion of the twentieth century and became the most protracted and bloodiest fighting of the Second World War.

Drawing on a superb collection of rare and unpublished German photographs accompanied by in-depth captions and text, this book reveals the invasion from the day the Wehrmacht rolled forward across the Soviet frontier in June 1941, until it finally stalled in the depths of the worst Russian winter for more than fifty years.

The objective of Barbarossa was for the German forces to crush the Soviet war machine and infrastructure of the country, and to swiftly advance and capture Leningrad, Moscow and the Ukraine using tried and tested Blitzkrieg tactics. Hitler believed that Barbarossa would be completed by October 1941, and it was for that reason alone his troops were not prepared for winter combat. Yet, the Wehrmacht knew little about their enemy, and were shocked by the vast distances in which their foot soldiers and machines had to march. Although the initial stages of the campaign went exceedingly well, enemy resistance grew and the campaign soon turned into the greatest and longest land battle which mankind had ever fought. By the winter of 1941, Russia was still unconquered and the losses in men and equipment were immense. Barbarossa had effectively failed, and the deep scars left by that first winter on the Eastern Front would be carried by the German soldier until the very end of the war.

During the morning of 22 June 1941 troops prepare to move East in a variety of infantry trucks and Horch cross-country vehicles. Note the MG34 machine gun mounted on a Dreibein 34 anti-aircraft tripod mount. It is fitted with a 50-round belt drum magazine.

Chapter I

Invasion Unleashed

For the invasion of Russia, code-named Barbarossa, the German Army assembled some three million men, divided into a total of 105 infantry divisions and 32 panzer divisions. There were 3,332 tanks, over 7,000 artillery pieces, 60,000 motor vehicles and 625,000 horses. This massive force was distributed into three army groups: Army Group North, commanded by General Wilhelm Ritter von Leeb, had assembled its forces in East Prussia on the Lithuanian frontier. His force provided the main spearhead for the advance on Leningrad.

Army Group Centre, commanded by General Fedor von Bock, assembled on the 1939 Polish/Russian Frontier, both north and south of Warsaw. Bock's force consisted of 42 infantry divisions of the 4. and 9.Armee and Panzergruppen.II and III. This army contained the largest number of German infantry and Panzer divisions in all three army groups.

Army Group South, commanded by Field Marshal Gerd von Rundstedt was deployed down the longest stretch of the border with Russia. The front, reaching from central Poland to the Black Sea, was held by one Panzergruppe, three German and two Rumanian armies, plus a Hungarian motorised corps, all under German command.

During the early morning of 22 June 1941, the German Army finally unleashed the maelstrom that was Barbarossa. Both the infantry and panzer divisions wasted no time and soon sliced through the bewildered Russian forces on every front. The ferocity and effectiveness of both the infantry and panzer divisions were so great that some of the Red Army forces they surrounded were gigantic. Groups of up to fifteen Russia divisions were trapped at a time and slowly and systematically annihilated in a hurricane of fire.

The strongest army group, Army Group Centre, made a series of heavy penetrating drives through the Russian heartlands, bulldozing through the marshy ground to the main Russian defences. Within days of its first attacks across the frontier both the infantry and panzer divisions had pulverized bewildered Russian formations, which led to a string of victories along its entire front.

On the northern front, Leeb's Army Group North was driving its forces at tremendous speed. It was given the task of destroying the Red Army fighting in the Baltic region. Hitler stipulated on the eve of the invasion that the German objective was to thrust across East

Prussia, smashing Soviet positions along the Baltic, liquidating the bases of the Baltic Fleet, destroying what was left of Russian naval power and capturing Kronstadt and Leningrad. Once the city had been razed to the ground, the German armies could sweep down from the north while the main force closed in on Moscow from the west. With half a million men at Leeb's disposal, comprising almost 30 divisions, six of them armoured and motorized with 1,500 Panzers and 12,000 heavy weapons, plus an air fleet of nearly 1,000 planes, he was determined to strike along the Baltic coast and dispose of the Russian force once and for all.

Leeb's rapid two-pronged offensive along the Baltic opened up at first light on the morning of 22 June 1941. His force, consisting of 16th and 18th Armies, smashed through the Soviet defences. Russian soldiers stood helpless in its path, too shocked to take action. Over the next weeks to come, German troops of Army Group North continued to chew through enemy positions heading through Lithuania, Latvia and Estonia, straight towards their objective – Leningrad. Fortunately, the earth was baked under the blistering summer heat and Leeb's army was able to advance rapidly through the Baltic states.

An excellent photograph showing a multitude of support vehicles along a road crossing into Russia during the morning of 22 June 1941. The letter 'G' painted in white on the rear of the vehicles indicates that they belong to General Guderian's Panzergruppe II. The bulk of an infantry division rode in trucks, cars, wagons, and carts or on horses, bicycles and motorcycles, but its rifle companies walked.

A German infantry division's rifle company walking to battle. The weather is warm as many of the troops have rolled-up their tunic sleeves to try and keep cool whilst on the move. Attached to their black leather infantryman's belt is the M1935 steel helmet.

Opposite: Infantry march along a road during the opening phase of 'Barbarossa'. These soldiers are equipped with the web battle pack carrier to which was attached their mess kit, shelter cape, and other important equipment. Note the loaf of bread secured on the infantryman's back. All of the soldiers wear the standard M1936 service uniform with the black leather infantry man's belt. Attached to the belt they wear their rifle ammunition pouches for their Karabiner 98K bolt action rifle.

A flak crew can be seen towing their 2cm FlaK gun on its limber along a road destined for the front lines. In combat these limbers would stay relatively close to the gun just in case the weapon was needed to be rapidly re-positioned.

Opposite: A photograph taken the moment a 21cm Mrs18 Morser opens fire against an enemy target. These weapons were purposely designed to fire projectiles at higher than normal angles of elevation for long-range firing. They could inflict considerable damage on enemy lines and were used extensively on the eastern front to destroy fortifications, bunker systems and any other enemy defensive position.

Infantry on the move passing a small lake during the early phase of the operation in the East. Note the soldier or range-taker carrying an optical range finder. The optical range finder was used to determine the range of an enemy target so that a FlaK crew could be more accurate when firing.

Two medium inflatable pneumatic boats in undergrowth with a smaller boat. These pneumatic boats were quite capable of carrying more than two tons of cargo between them. Note the MG34 machine gun resting in one of the boats with two MG ammunition cases.

A 2cm FlaK 38 gunner has elevated his barrel toward the sky. The crew of a gun like this normally comprised of the commander, gun-layer, range-taker, range-setter, loader and ammunition handler. When this weapon was fired the spent cartridge cases were ejected from the right side. Sometimes a rod and net device was fitted to catch them.

A light Horch cross-country vehicle belonging to Guderian's Panzergruppe moves through a captured village following an Sd.Kfz.232 radio vehicle with long range antennae. These armoured cars were intended for reconnaissance and screening. They scouted ahead of mechanized units to assess enemy strength and location. Their primary role was to observe rather than fight enemy units, although they were expected to fight enemy reconnaissance elements when required.

A 3.7cm PaK 35/36 gun is being towed by a Krupp-Protz Kfz.81 armoured car. A typical infantry regiment controlled three infantry battalions, an infantry gun company with six 7.5cm l.IG18 and two 15cm s.IG33 guns, and an anti-tank company with twelve 3.7cm PaK 35/36 guns.

Here a well concealed 10.5cm gun is being prepared for firing on a target during operations on the eastern front in June 1941. The gunner is looking through the gun sight in order to give the crew accurate information relating to the correct range and elevation needed to fire the gun.

One of the quickest and most effective means of moving vast amounts of equipment from one part of the front to another was by rail. Here in this photograph artillery limbers are being transported to the front. In Russia the bulk of all motive power was undertaken by animal draughts and thousands of caissons and other pieces of equipment were required to support the drive East.

Horse-drawn infantry pass wreckage. A Soviet tank track lays strewn next to a dirt track alongside other destroyed pieces of equipment. Spent Russian shell cartridges can be seen scattered among the remains of the decimated enemy position.

Here a camouflaged 15cm howitzer is being towed by animal draught. The 15cm gun was broken down into two loads, and each drawn by six horses. In this photograph the carriage and mounting are seen with equipment secured to the gun trails. The gun's tube and breech were transported on a special four-wheeled wagon.

Along the frontier these artillery troops are armed with a 10.5cm le.FH16 light field howitzer. The wheels on the artillery piece consisted of a heavy duty cast steel with a solid rubber rim. This type of design allowed the gun to be towed at relatively high-speed by a motorized vehicle.

Three photographs showing three different positions of an MG34 machine gun with 50-round belt drum magazine and an anti-aircraft ring sight mounted on a Dreifuss 34 anti-aircraft tripod. Throughout the war support units were issued with light machine guns for self-defence and were able to counter low flying enemy aircraft quite regularly.

A soldier surveys the battlefield through a pair of 6x30 binoculars. Secured inside his black leather infantryman's leather belt are two M1924 stick grenades. Note the foliage attached to his M1935 steel helmet, which is secured by a black rubber band.

An unidentified unit in a small encampment just outside a village. The soldiers have used a number of shelter quarters for housing troops. These field tents were of standard design and had a fly tarp erected over it to provide insulation from the sun in order to reduce intensive heat inside the tent. These shelter quarter encampments could be quickly erected by the troops, and were an important part in a soldiers training.

Heavily equipped infantry move along a dirt road with a medical vehicle in support approaching an abandoned Soviet bunker position. A German grave can be seen freshly dug at the side of the track, probably a fatality trying to capture the Russian position. A PaK 35/36 can be seen on the road without its crew, evidence of heavy fighting and loss of life.

Six photographs showing Russian PoWs. The German drive through Russia in June and July 1941 was so swift that the Russian Army was completely taken by surprise. As a result many thousands of troops were quickly surrounded and decimated. Those remnants that survived either tried to escape or were captured. These four photographs show Russian PoWs grouped together awaiting a fate that can only be imagined. The bulk of the Russian PoWs that survived in the prison camps in the East were transported to Poland and Germany where they were put to work in concentration camps. By 1942, many were working in the armaments industry in appalling conditions. The majority did not survive.

Here in this photograph Russian male civilians have been herded together by Wehrmacht troops and are probably going to be pressed into service as work gangs, aiding the German advance. Many were employed as forced labour to maintain lines of communications and unload supplies.

An officer jokes with a soldier holding the rank of an Obergefreiter. Both are standing next to a knocked out soviet tank that has been blown on its side by the impact of the explosion. They wear the M36 field blouse with its distinctive dark-green facing collar. His M40 type service trousers are tucked into a pair of marching boots.

Infantrymen march passed a knocked out Soviet KV-IIA heavy tank. This massive tank was armed with a 152mm M-1938/40 L/20 howitzer in a high, box turret with all-round traverse, on the KV-I hull. In spite of the impressive fire-power the vehicle was notoriously unreliable in the summer defensive campaigns of 1941. As a result the KV-II was soon removed from combat duties after the first summer operations against the Germans.

An infantryman leads a small column of dejected Soviet prisoners across a field. There were two reasons for the Soviet Army being caught in a state of unpreparedness. Many of the Red Army troops lacked the proper war experience compared to the Germans. Another was that the old border fortifications along the Soviet frontier were still incomplete, and as a direct result the Russians were unable to hold a defensive line for any appreciable length of time.

A 3.7cm PaK35/37 anti-tank gun crew has moved their weapon onto a road in a state of readiness. A typical infantry regiment controlled three infantry battalions, an infantry gun company with six 7.5cm l.IG18 and two 15cm s.IG33 guns, and an anti-tank company with twelve 3.7cm PaK35/36 guns.

Waffen-SS troops from the famous Das Reich Division round up female Russian prisoners. Contrary to popular belief there were no all-female combat troops in the Soviet Army. The majority of women in the Russian Army served as snipers, anti-aircraft units, medical duties, signallers, traffic controllers, and only a few ever fought in ground combats.

One of the most effective forms of observation, apart from flying, was to use an observation balloon. Here in these two photographs taken in sequence is an artillery observation battery utilising a balloon in a remote area. With almost no enemy aircraft balloon observation could be undertaken with little concern. However, it was still vulnerable to attack as the balloon was hydrogen-filled. Normally two men were sent-up in the balloon basket, one to record data and relay it to the ground by telephone, whilst the other was the observer, who would keep a lookout for the approach of any enemy aircraft.

A group of Wehrmacht motorcyclists pause during their long drive east. They can all be seen wearing the double-breasted rubberized motorcycle coat. The garment was waterproof and was worn with army issue canvas leather gloves or cloth mittens, with overshoe leggings or army boots. One of the hazards of travelling by motorcycle, especially in the Soviet Union, was the lack of good-quality roads for vehicles. Motorcyclists that decided to avoid the roads and travel cross-country often found it a perilous undertaking, and the casualty rate among motorcyclists was inevitably high.

What appears to be a forward artillery observation post and an observer estimates the range to a target using a 6x30 Sf 14Z Scherenfernrohr (scissor binoculars). Although the observer was primarily tasked with detecting targets, they also looked for weapon muzzles, moving infantry, armoured vehicles, fires, smoke from cooking and anything else they could detect to find and locate their enemy.

In the summer heat a group of shirtless signalmen pose for the camera next to a tent. Parked nearby is a radio vehicle fitted with long-range antennae.

A signalman on a field telephone. A signals battalion provided field telephone and radio communications support within a German division, and linked all subordinate units. Telephone and radio troops had switchboards and laid wires and cables for telephone communications and communicated with corps headquarters.

A photograph taken from the rear of a vehicle, possibly from a Horch Cross Country car. It shows four motorcyclists following the column as it passes a line of Soviet PoWs being escorted to the rear along a road. A motorcycle combination escorts the PoWs to the rear.

A 15cm s.FH18 being prepared for firing. This weapon was the standard piece in a division and employment of artillery was a necessity to any ground force engaging an enemy. Both infantry and motorized artillery regiments became the backbone of the fighting in the early years on the Russian front.

In one of a number of shelters erected along the front in Army Group North. Although such shelters did not provide much in terms of protection for the men against heavy enemy fire, they certainly provided the soldiers with adequate shelter against the bitter elements.

During a pause in the march Landser rest before resuming another very long march east. Many of the soldiers that entered Russia during the summer of 1941 were totally surprised by the vastness of the country and the amount of time it took to reach one objective after another. For many men the drive was arduous and exhausting.

An unlimbered 10.5cm l.FH18 field howitzer in undergrowth is being loaded ready for a fire mission. The 10.5cm field howitzer provided the division with a relatively effective mobile base of fire. It was primarily the artillery regiments that were given the task of destroying enemy positions and fortified defences and conducting counter-battery fire prior to an armoured assault.

A mortar crew prepare their leGrW36 mortar for action. The intended role for the leGrW36 was to engage pockets of resistance that were beyond the range of hand grenades. It was designed for high angled fire only (no less than 42°). The main drawbacks of the weapon were its inadequate range and the limited effectiveness of its ammunition, which was regarded as not heavy enough.

Infantry with their commanding officer pause in a field during the initial stages of the campaign. The support vehicle is heavily camouflaged in order to try and break-up its distinctive shape from both aerial and ground attack.

The crew of a well-concealed 10.5cm l.FH18 pose for the camera during a pause in firing. This gun was the workhorse of the German artillery regiments. The 10.5cm field howitzer provided the division with a relatively effective mobile base of fire. It was primarily the artillery regiments that were given the task of destroying enemy positions and fortified defences and conducting counter-battery fire prior to an armoured assault.

Mountain or Gebirgsjäger troops in the process of crossing a river with their pack animal. The mule was the Gebirgs main source of transporting equipment to the front across all types of terrain. These hardy pack animals were better suited for rough terrain than horses and were used extensively by the mountain soldiers throughout the war.

At the side of the road in a field horses towing a HF 12 small kitchen wagon pause in the long march and graze. These small mobile kitchens could also operate on the move, cooking stews, soups, and coffee. The limber carried utensils and equipment. In the distance other horses can be seen resting as a convoy of support vehicles wind along the dusty road bound for the front.

A very well concealed 10.5cm l.FH18 covered with saplings overlooks enemy positions. The heat during the summer of 1941 on the Eastern Front was oppressive and in order to cool down this artilleryman has discarded his uniform completely. His M1935 steel helmet can be seen on the gun trail so that at a moment's notice he could wear it if his gun was called into action.

A forward observation post and signalmen seen with cable reels and two field telephones. From this post the relay post could talk to its platoons and the battalion headquarters, which would have to relay messages from adjacent companies. The signals soldier was nicknamed the 'line puller' or 'Strippenzieher'.

Infantrymen move forward towards a burning position. Note how the soldiers advance along the side of the road, which was a precaution against enemy aerial attacks. On the other side of the road a Horch Cross country car towing a trailer full of supplies has halted along with motorcycle combinations.

With typical German military thoroughness last minute checks are made to halftracks that are secured to flatbed rail cars destined for the front lines in Russia. Many thousands of vehicles were transported to the East this way, which not only saved considerable time and effort, but reduced wear and tear.

Vehicles and cyclists cross a heavy pontoon bridge known by the Germans as a Brückengerät B. The pontoon boats have been lashed together and the bridging deck sections secured over them in order to allow traffic and soldiers on foot to pass over.

A battery of 15cm heavy field howitzers in a field being prepared for action. They have been purposely placed on the edge of a wood in order to afford some degree of concealment from aerial or ground surveillance.

A soldier poses for the camera inside a dug-out which is probably a forward observation post. Placed around his position are two M1924 stick grenades, 6x30 field binocular case, gas mask canister, the 9mm Bergmann MP28 machine pistol and his 6x30 field binoculars.

One of the most important ways to maintain the morale of any soldier on the battlefield was through his stomach. Here in this photograph kitchen staff prepare food for the men. The troops nicknamed these kitchen wagons as 'goulash cannons'. Many of these mobile kitchens were often towed by animal draught.

A divisional bridge column of motor vehicles awaits the signal to advance on a road that has been cleared of destroyed Soviet weapons. The Bussing and Henschel trucks are towing bridge equipment 'T' Type 1 pontoon trailers.

A heavy MG34 machine gun position on a sustained fire-mount overlooking an enemy position. A well-sighted, well-hidden and well-supplied MG34 could hold up an entire attacking regiment. This machine gun is perfectly sighted, and could inflict heavy losses on an enemy advance. Throughout the summer campaign and indeed for the rest of the war the MG34 had tremendous staying power against enemy infantry, and troops continuously deployed their machine guns in the most advantageous defensive and offensive positions.

Infantry and vehicles in the process of crossing a combination fixed-type and pontoon bridge. This combination was normally employed when the bottom was too shallow to float pontoon boats. Note the film camera on a tripod mounted on a Horch Cross Country car. It appears that the crossing of the bridge has been staged for film. Thousands of hours of film were recorded during the victorious march of the Wehrmacht into Russia, and these were shown on news reels in cinemas throughout the Reich.

Chapter II
Summer Battles

The ultimate objective of Army Group Centre was to drive as rapidly as possible eastwards to the city of Smolensk, which commanded the road to the Russian capital, Moscow. Facing this impressive array of German might along the River Dnieper and Dvina were groups of heavily defended fortifications called the Stalin Line. The defenders were the Russian 13th Army of the Western Front, and the 20th Army, 21st Army and the 22nd Army of the Supreme Command (STAVKA) Reserve. In the region around the strategic city of Vitebsk the 19th Army was ordered to hold at all costs, while the 16th Army was hastily moved in front of Smolensk. It was the threat in the north from 3rd Panzer Army and 39th Panzer Corps that seriously worried the Red Army. However, in spite of this concern Stalin had called for a Great Patriotic War against the Nazi invader, and every soldier was determined to do his duty and hold his position to the death. As Army Group Centre continued a general push towards Smolensk in early July 1941, the Russians began a more determined defence. Many bridges were blown up and, for the first time, the Red Army units began laying mines to slow down the Germans. To make matters worse for both the infantry and panzer divisions heavy rain, typical for July in central Russia, suddenly began turning the roads into streaming rivers of mud, and advancing German units found themselves either slowing down to a painful snail's pace or totally immobile for hours at a time.

The German delays gave the Soviets time to organize for a massive armoured counter blow.

On 6 July, the Russians finally launched their attack in front of Smolensk with the Soviet 20th Army's 7th and 5th Mechanized Corps attacking advancing German troops and armour with 700 tanks. What followed was the battle of Smolensk with Red Army infantry bitterly contesting every part of ground along the Dnieper River.

In spite of relatively strong Russian defensive positions, by the second week of July the 3rd. Panzergruppe's 20th Panzer Division established a bridgehead on the east bank of the River Dvina and threatened Vitebsk. To the south, away from the main crossings, Panzergruppe.II launched surprise attacks, forcing the River Dnieper. The Soviet 13th Army was pushed back, losing 5 divisions. As both German panzer armies drove east, three Soviet Armies, the 20th, 19th and 16th faced the prospect of encirclement around Smolensk.

What followed was intensive fighting. Armour and troops from the 29th Motorized Infantry Division in a series of successive attacks blasted its way through towards the city. Soviet soldiers either fought to the death or saved themselves by escaping the impending slaughter by withdrawing to another makeshift position. During the early morning of 16 July fighting intensified with even greater losses to the Russians. The battles that took place in and around Smolensk became a fierce contest of attrition, and although the Russians showed great fortitude and determination, they were constantly hampered by lack of weapons and manpower needed to sustain them on the battlefield. Consequently, the remaining troops holding out in the city were subjected to merciless ground and aerial bombardments. The situation for the defenders looked grim. The ferocity of the German attack was immense and without respite. After nearly twenty-four hours of almost continuous battle the Russian soldiers had become exhausted. Stalin's insistence that his troops must fight from fixed positions without any tactical retreat had consequently caused many units to become encircled, leaving tank units to speed past unhindered and achieve even deeper penetrations.

By the early afternoon of 16 July Smolensk was finally captured by 29th Motorized Infantry Division. In the north, Hoth's Panzergruppe.III was moving much more slowly. The terrain was swampy and the rain was still hampering operations in a number of places. The Russians were fighting desperately to escape the trap that was developing. On 18 July, the great armoured pincers of the two German panzer armies came within 10 miles of closing the gap. But the jaws would not snap shut and bitter fighting raged for more than a week.

While the battle of Smolensk raged and the Germans tried liquidating the Smolensk pocket with some 500,000 Soviet troops fighting inside, General Guderian immediately set about implementing plans to crush Soviet forces further east around the town of Roslavl. The operation had taken the Red Army by complete surprise. The sudden speed and depth of the German attack was a brilliant display of all-arms coordination. The Soviets were quite unprepared for the might of the German attack. In some areas along the front units were simply brushed aside and totally destroyed. Red Army survivors recalled that they had been caught off guard, lulled into a false sense of security after escaping from the Smolensk pocket. Now they were being attacked by highly mobile armour and blasted by heavy artillery. In many places the force of attack was so heavy that they were unable to organize any type of defence. In total confusion, hundreds of troops, disheartened and frightened, retreated to avoid the slaughter, whilst other more fanatical units remained, ruthlessly defending their positions to the death. On 1 August, Guderian's force launched his Roslavl offensive. The Russian force that was thrown in against the German attack was

Two photographs showing mortar crew armed with a 5cm leGrW36 mortar. The 5cm leichte Granatwerfer 36 or leGrW 36 (light grenade-launcher model 1936) was not a widely used weapon on the eastern front in 1941. The weapon was complicated, not very powerful and lacked range. In relation to its poor performance, the mortar was expensive to make. By 1941, it was slowly withdrawn from front-line service.

remnants from the battle of Smolensk. They were completely exhausted, short of ammunition and vulnerable.

The Russians tried desperately to hold on to the town of Roslavl, but under direct attack by seven fresh German infantry divisions, the defence soon crumbled away. Around the town a pocket soon began to form, with Germans bringing up greater artillery concentration, whilst Red Army troops feebly trying to break out. Roslavl finally fell to the Germans on 3 August. Guderian immediately ordered a panzer striking force of three divisions away from the main battle to probe southwards and clear up stragglers from both Smolensk and Roslavl.

The battles of Smolensk and Roslavl was one of the swiftest as well as one of the most complete German Army victories in the East. Altogether some 300,000 Soviet soldiers had been captured in the Smolensk pocket. However, 200,000 had managed to break out and fight in Roslavl and surrounding areas further east.

As Army Group Centre pushed ever deeper into the Soviet heartlands, by mid-July Army Group North had broken through south of Pskov and rolled toward Luga. At the rate they were advancing, they would need no more than nine or ten days to reach the outskirts of Leningrad. But following their surge of success, the Wehrmacht were losing momentum. Not only were their supply lines being overstretched, but enemy resistance began to stiffen on the road to Leningrad. In a desperate attempt to blunt the German advance and prevent them from reaching the imperial city, brigades of Russian marines, naval units, and more than 80,000 men from the Baltic Fleet were hastily sent into action against Leeb's forces. These Russian soldiers were now the sole barrier between Leningrad and the Germans. Although the advance was hampered by these Russian forces, by the end of August 1941, Leeb's panzers were finally within sight of Leningrad. The terrified civilians left inside the city walls were now going to endure one of the most brutal sieges in 20th century history.

As the summer of 1941 passed and the Germans drew closer to the city gates, the citizens of Leningrad were given the grim orders to defend their city to the death. Although Leeb's forces had arrived within shelling distance of Leningrad, the advance had not gone as planned. Already units had been badly disrupted and were mired on the Leningrad Front by stiffening resistance. Even Leeb himself was now under considerable pressure from Hitler to complete his assignment of encircling Leningrad, to join forces with the Finns, and to wipe out the Baltic Fleet. His forces were desperately needed for the Moscow Front, where the Wehrmacht was preparing to go in for the kill and capture the capital. But despite assurances from Leeb that his forces were making good progress, German troops were still entangled in hundreds of miles of earth walls, anti-tank ditches and wire barricades, thousands of defensive pill-boxes, and the harrying activities of Russian tanks outside Leningrad.

Here a 21cm Mrs18 is being served by its crew prior to firing. One of the guns 21cm projectiles is being displayed for the camera. This weapon was the largest calibre artillery piece to see action with the Wehrmacht and Waffen-SS. The gun was purposely designed to fire projectiles at higher than normal angles of elevation for long-range firing.

By 17 September, the Moscow Front could wait no longer for victory in the north. The powerful 41st Panzer Corps, which Leeb required to sledge-hammer his way to the outskirts of Leningrad, was taken out of the line and ordered to the Moscow Front. Without the 41st Panzer Corps the whole dynamic of Army Group North had altered. There would now be no attack on Leningrad. Instead, Hitler ordered that the city would be encircled and the inhabitants defending inside would be starved to death.

Meanwhile on the Southern Front Rundstedt's six German infantry divisions with some six hundred tanks distributed among them were continuing to bulldoze their way through weakly held Russian defences. The main thrust in the south was directed between the southern edge of the Pripet Marshes and the foothills of the Carpathian Mountains. Here

A 21cm Mrs18 on its gun carriage being readied by the crew. This heavy mortar large-calibre gun had a range of almost 17 km, the large calibre and its enormously effective fire made the mortar a very effective artillery weapon. Although it was hindered by its weight of some 16.7 tons it remained in service until the end of the war. It was widely used destroying enemy fortifications and well dug-in positions.

Rundstedt concentrated the whole of the 1st Panzer Army, 6th Army, and 17th Army. The 6th Army under the faithful command of Field-Marshal von Reichenau consisted of three Army Corps, XVII, XVII, XXXXIV, and one reserve, the LV Army Corps. Reichenau had commanded the 6th Army during the battle of France in 1940, but the army had already made a name for itself during the invasion of Poland. On the Eastern Front the 6th Army once again completely mastered the enemy despite being continually harassed by strong Russian forces that had been cut off in the wooded swampland between the Pripet Marshes and the Carpathian Mountains. As the 6th Army pushed on towards the Dnieper River its primary task was to hold on to as much ground as possible and prevent all intact retreating enemy formations from withdrawing deep into Russia. Over the next days and weeks that followed the speed of the 6th Army was multiplied tenfold by the mobility of the Southern Army group's armour as it rammed and overrun enemy obstacles. Again and again the Russians were overwhelmed by the German onslaught. By August the 6th Army had swung out east of Kiev as German forces began mopping up the last remnants in and around the besieged city. When the battle of Kiev finally ended on 21 September 1941 almost 665,000 Russian troops had been captured in the encirclement. Exhilarated by the fall of Kiev, the 6th Army mercilessly pushed forward, leaving a trail of devastation in its wake. Across the whole of Reichenau's front tanks hammered deeper, and the guns of the infantry divisions lengthened their range. For the troops of the 6th Army it seemed that Blitzkrieg had once again been imprinted on the battlefield and there was an aura of invincibility among the men.

An interesting photograph showing both Wehrmacht and Luftwaffe in a field. A FlaK38 is manned by a full crew and soldiers and Luftwaffe personnel survey the battlefield for enemy movement. Note the 7.9mm MG30(t) on its bipod. This machine gun was of Czech origin and was used by the Wehrmacht during the early part of the war on the Eastern Front.

Advancing through a decimated city in the area of Army Group Centre in July 1941 an Sd.Kfz.10/4 mounting a 2cm FlaK30 gun leads a column of Horch cross-country cars. The sides of the halftrack are folded up with additional magazine cases attached. These sides could be folded down to allow extra space on board the halftrack for the flak crew. Note the national flag draped over the front of the bonnet for aerial recognition.

Infantrymen seen next to a Fieseler Fi 156 Storch reconnaissance aircraft. The Storch's ability for STOL (Short Take Off and Landing) made it ideal for crude battlefield locations. Its small wingspan, fixed leading edge slats and slotted aileron flaps (which extended the length of the wing) allowed the Storch to take off in as little as 200 feet in a light head wind, and only needed 70 feet of runway to land.

A halftrack was mainly used to tow various ordnance from one part of the front to another. However, it was also utilized for other tasks such as towing other vehicles that had developed mechanical failure or pulling trailers full of heavy supplies, as in this photograph.

A Pz.Kpfw.III rolls along a road somewhere on the eastern front. During the opening stages of the campaign, there were some 956 Pz.Kpfw.III's. This was by far the largest contingent of armour to fight in the war thus far. Although the Pz.Kpfw.III was very successful the eventual distances which had to be covered limited its tactics, as well as causing breakdowns and immense supply problems.

The crew of a 2cm flak gun train their weapon against an enemy target. This weapon was very effective and had a fire rate of 120 – 280 rounds per minute. Strong anti-aircraft defences only came into prominence from September 1941, as the Soviet Air Force started to inflict heavy casualties on German divisions.

An excellent photograph of an 8cm sGrW 34 mortar crew. The position is well concealed in a field and the weapon camouflaged by Zeltbahn, which blends well with the local terrain. Each battalion fielded six of these excellent 8cm sGrW 34 mortars, which could fire 15 mortar projectiles per minute to a range of 2,625 yards.

Soldiers frisk captured Soviet troops for hidden weapons. Various papers and other personal effects are removed before they are marched off to the rear. During the summer of 1941 many hundreds of thousands of Red Army troops were captured by the Germans. In the Uman Pocket for instance some 100,000 prisoners, over 300 tanks and 850 guns were captured by the Germans.

An Sd.Kfz.221 light armoured reconnaissance vehicle advances beside a railway line. The Sdkfz. 221 was armed with a 7.9mm MG34 machine gun, manned by a two man crew, and had 4-wheel drive. Armour protection was originally 8mm thick, but increased to 14.5 mm on later models.

An infantryman surveys some of the damage to a Russian position. Among the wreckage is a destroyed Soviet 85mm Model 1939 anti-aircraft gun. This weapon was introduced in early 1940, and although designed primarily as an anti-aircraft gun, like the German 8.8cm, it was widely used in the anti-tank role. The gun was fitted with semi automatic breech mechanism and a large multi-baffle muzzle brake to reduce recoil and increase the muzzle velocity.

At an encampment somewhere on the eastern front are a number of vehicles including infantry support trucks, Horch cross-country cars and prime movers towing 8.8cm FlaK guns. Note the national flag draped on the bonnet of the staff car.

A signalman operating a portable radio. This device was the standard radio used at battalion and regimental level. These widely used portable radios were carried by a soldier on a specially designed back-pack frame, and when connected to each other (upper and lower valves) via special cables, could be used on the march.

A Luftwaffe FlaK crew limbering up their 8.8cm FlaK gun somewhere on the Eastern Front. This flak gun was used in two roles, one as a mobile heavy anti-aircraft battery, and also in a more static role for defence against aerial attacks. In this latter role the guns were arranged into large batteries directed by a single controller, and were moved only rarely.

Infantry stopped in a forest somewhere in Army Group Centre in the summer of 1941. A commanding officer can be seen on horseback passing the group of soldiers, two of which are armed with an MG34 machine gun. One of the soldiers can be seen with a mosquito net attached to his M1938 field cap. Mosquitoes were very problematic in the Russian swamps, especially in the early summer. In a drastic attempt to repel the insects from biting many troops took to wearing mosquito-nets over their heads.

A Luftwaffe telephone relay post on the frontline. One of the signalmen can be seen speaking on a field telephone. He is more than likely relaying a message back to his command centre with important data on enemy location or strength.

Russian civilians are put to work digging a river bank where an old wooden bridge once stood. Approaching the workforce is a motorcyclist wearing his familiar rubberized water proof motorcycle coat.

A horse-drawn A HF 12 field kitchen wagon (Feldküchenwagen) advances along a typical Russian road. The long distances which the horses had to travel can well be imagined, but generally, in spite of being under battle conditions, the horses were relatively well cared for.

Soldiers converse after disembarking from an infantry support truck. A typical infantry division consisted of three infantry regiments, an artillery regiment, reconnaissance, anti-tank, pioneer, and signal battalions, plus divisional services. Trucks transported much of the supporting battalions, but there were many infantry units, that marched on foot, including all the supply columns that were horse-drawn.

Opposite: This Gebirgsjäger radioman can be seen with a Tornisterfunkgerät b1 (Torn. Fu. b1 (S/E)), or "pack radio". These portable radio sets were widely used during the war and could be carried in two parts by the radiomen on specially designed back-pack frames.

A close-up image of a motorcyclist wearing a pair of goggles in order to avoid getting dust and other foreign matter in the eyes. He also wears the M1938 field cap and M1936 field blouse.

Infantry keep low beside a road due to heavy enemy activity. In the distance rising smoke indicates possible heavy fighting in the area. The soldiers are armed with the Karabiner98K bolt-action rifle.

A forward observation post somewhere in Army Group South during the summer of 1941. A Zeltbahn shelter quarter protects this crude shelter from the wind and rain. Note the antennae for Tornisterfunkgerät b1 (Torn. Fu. b1 (S/E)) radio pack.

Horse drawn infantry advance along a road towards a captured town in Army Group North. For the invasion of the Soviet Union the Wehrmacht had become entirely dependent on nearly one million horses. However, by the end of the summer some 1000 horses died each day on average during the war in Russia. Consequently, a vast amount of organization was required for the rapid replacement of animals, and this fell to the already overstretched support services.

Infantry wearing their greatcoats take-up positions inside a Soviet tank ditch as they advance towards Kiev in late August 1941. In August, Hitler had made his decision that Moscow would no longer be the primary objective. Instead he was determined to take the Ukraine with all its wealth in food production, minerals, ores and factories. It was for this reason that Kiev was to be taken at all costs.

Two photographs, one taken out in a field and the other in a forest, showing shelter quarters being put together by the Landser to construct pup-tents. This water resistant Zeltbahn could easily be joined together with one or three others to make two and four-man tents.

A photograph captures the moment a 10.5cm le.FH16 light field howitzer fires a projectile against an enemy target. It was primarily the artillery regiments that were given the task of destroying enemy positions and fortified defences and conducting counter-battery fire prior to an armoured or infantry assault.

Horse drawn supplies including a mobile field kitchen advance along a dusty road. Even by the time the Germans attacked the Soviet Union almost three quarters of a million horses alone were used in the early stages of the campaign. Although a great number carried soldiers and towed artillery, these animals were also used to pull huge amounts of various supplies from one sector of the front to another.

Two photographs showing a battery of 15cm heavy field howitzers, one prior to going into action, and the other during a fire mission on the eastern front. As the standard heavy field howitzer in the Wehrmacht, the gun was very effective at clearing up heavily concentrated positions to let tanks and infantry pour through unhindered.

A column of infantry lorries bound for the front advance along a road. Mounted on the vehicles covered by tarpaulin are Dreibein 34 anti-aircraft tripod with attached MG34 machine guns. The letter 'K' painted on the rear of the vehicles indicates it belongs to Kleist's Panzergruppe I, which was attached to Field Marshal Gerd von Rundstedt's Army Group South. Panzergruppe I included the III, XIV and XLVIII Army Corps (mot.), with five panzer divisions and four motorized SS divisions.

Infantrymen cross a pontoon bridge all armed with the Karabiner 98K bolt action rifle. The soldiers have been issued with the standard M1936 field blouse with its typical dark-green facing collar. They have been issued the usual rifleman's equipment and weapons; the army enlisted man's leather belt, infantry leather support straps, two rifle pouches and a gas cape, and the M1935 steel helmet worn under battle conditions. Note the M1924 stick grenades attached to their belt.

Troops advance through a destroyed town following its capture. By the extent of damage to the buildings the Russians have obviously put up considerable resistance. As German troops edged deeper into the Soviet heartlands resistance began to increase, putting more strain on some of the more overstretched units.

Officers survey the battlefield. A pair of Sf14Z scissor binoculars can be seen in order to give the commanders a better view of the terrain ahead. These binoculars were nicknamed 'donkey ears' and were able to estimate ranges.

A well-concealed Gebirgsjäger forward observation post. It shows a soldier belonging to a signals battalion communicating on the telephone, whilst his assistant scribbles the information on a notepad. The signals battalion provided both field and radio communications support within the division, linking all subordinate units. Regiments and battalions had their own signals, but for internal communications. Telephone and radio troops were attached to all divisional units and laid wire and cable for telephone connections.

A 10.5cm le.FH18 howitzer in a field being prepared for firing. In total, the 10.5cm howitzer had a nine-man crew. Usually fewer men are seen serving this piece because often some of the crew were to the rear with the horses, limber and caisson.

Infantryman seen standing next to a knocked out Soviet T-34 tank. Other wreckage can also be seen tangled in the marshland. The great value of the T-34 was its simple design which made it easy to manufacture and easy to repair. The Russians could afford to lose many of these vehicles, in spite of the advancing Germans, as literally thousands of them were entering the battlefield quicker than the Germans could replace their own losses in armour.

A 10.5cm howitzer is loaded aboard a ship along the Baltic coast in the late summer of 1941. Although its destination is unknown, there were many shipments of supplies sent by sea from the homeland and the Baltic States to either Russia or Finland.

A 2cm FlaK crew preparing for action against an enemy target. A soldier can be seen with an optical range finder. The range finder was remarkably good at finding the initial range, but it needed operators with special aptitudes reinforced with constant training for them to keep track of the target during a battle.

As pioneers re-construct a damaged bridge a column of support vehicles uses a temporary light bridge section to bring additional supplies forward without hindering units up front that are fighting. Keeping frontline units re-supplied was a constant logistical nightmare for the Wehrmacht, and it often resulted in leading units grinding to a halt until additional supplies were brought up.

Two photographs showing German infantry with inflatable boats. One of the photographs shows pioneers preparing to press their boats into service at the side of a river bank. The other photo shows troops clambering into the inflatable boats. Two paddles either side was normally sufficient enough for the boats to be propelled through the water, even when carrying a full complement of infantry onboard with heavy weapons and equipment. Using inflatable boats was one of a number of methods to cross a river. They could be put into operation much quicker than a pontoon bridge, and were less vulnerable to attack than a fixed bridge.

A StuG.III.Ausf.B advances along a road bound for the front lines. For the invasion of Russia German factories were able to complete 548 StuG.III vehicles. The StuG had a crew of four and came equipped with a 7.5cm StuK 37 L/24 gun capable of traversing from 12.5 degrees left to 12.5 degrees right. With the vehicle's low silhouette for better survivability, it not only provided sterling offensive service, but fought brilliantly during defensive battles as well.

Infantrymen march through a destroyed town. The average German soldier had never experienced such long foot marches before. Much of their advance, especially in southern Russia comprised of vast open spaces, with huge areas of land devoid of any habitation. Often when soldiers arrived in a town or village they were either destroyed or the inhabitants had deserted in panic from the fighting.

One of the most vital commodities required for the survival of the German forces to sustain itself on the battlefield was fuel. Here in this photograph a Luftwaffe vehicle is being supplied with fuel. Pipes are being fed into a number of drums and pumped with fuel.

An injured soldier is being stretchered to a field hospital which is situated well to the division's rear. The medical service normally operated two medical companies to support frontline units. One company was horse drawn and the other motorized. The most seriously wounded would be evacuated to corps-level hospitals.

A typical German defensive position in Russia. Although unable to sustain heavy systematic bombardments from the enemy these positions offered the men some degree of shelter from the rain and later the snow. Many hundreds of these dug-outs were built on the Eastern Front and were commonly known by the Germans as small houses.

Infantry move along a typical road in the Soviet Union. It would only take a short down-pour of rain to turn this dry road into a quagmire, making movement for both horses and wheeled transport very difficult.

Infantry survey damage to a number of support vehicles in a forest clearing. An Sd.Kfz.10 can be seen halted next to the vehicles. By the appearance of the surrounding trees it is apparent that an enemy shell has landed somewhere in the vicinity, causing damage to the undergrowth and the vehicles.

Three infantrymen joke in front of the camera. The soldier in the middle has clearly been injured and a freshly applied bandaged can be seen on his chin. His comrade to his right jovially displays two M1924 stick grenades.

A Pz.Kpfw.III crosses a combination fixed-type and pontoon bridge. The primary task of the Pz.Kpfw.III was to fight other tanks. However, although it was well built, in terms of armour, armament and mobility, it was not outstanding.

Two Pz.Kpfw.II's advance along a road. During the summer of 1941 the Pz.Kpfw.II demonstrated that this light tank was so seriously under-gunned and under-armoured that it could not fight effectively on the Eastern Front.

A column of Pz.Kpfw.38 (t) tanks advance through a captured Russian town. In the summer of 1941 the Panzer divisions relied heavily on the lighter tanks such as the Pz.Kpfw.38 (t) to provide the armoured punch necessary to break through enemy lines. Consequently, by late summer this put an increasing strain on the light tanks, and as a result many of them were either destroyed or developed mechanical problems.

The crew of a Pz.Kpfw.38 (t) pose for the camera. Note the divisional insignia painted on the turret in yellow indicating that it belongs to the 12th Panzer Division. In July, 1941, the 12th Panzer was moved to the Eastern Front and took part in operations to encircle Minsk, cross the Dnieper and to take Smolensk. The division was then shifted to Army Group North where it successfully fought in the Battle of Mga. However, it suffered heavy losses during the Soviet Winter counter-offensive north of Leningrad.

Vehicles belonging to Guderian's Panzergruppe II seen crossing an intact bridge as the column makes its way deeper into enemy territory. Note the divisional insignia painted in yellow on the rear of the light Horch Cross Country cars mud guard indicating that it belongs to the 13th Panzer Division.

Somewhere in Army Group South and troops rest in a field. An MG34 mounted on a Dreibein 34 antiaircraft tripod mount can be seen with its gunner, who is sleeping nearby. A motorcycle combination and a number of Horch Cross Country cars can be seen purposely spaced out across the field in order to reduce heavy loss to its column if there was an aerial attack.

An interesting photograph showing four inflatable boats ferrying a Pz.Kpfw.I across a river. This type of maneuver was seldom undertaken as it was often quite dangerous to move heavy armoured vehicles like this across a river without them becoming unstable.

What appears to be a forward artillery observation post and an observer estimates the range to a target using a 6x30 Sf 14Z Scherenfernrohr (scissor binoculars). Although the observer was primarily tasked with detecting targets, they also looked for weapon muzzles, moving infantry, armoured vehicles, fires, smoke from cooking and anything else they could detect to find and locate the enemy. Note the MG34 machine gun on a sustained fire mount overlooking an enemy target.

Two photographs showing Soviet PoWs rounded up during German operations in the Smolensk region in Army Group Centre. In spite of the huge amounts of prisoners captured during this operation the Russian 4th, 6th, 13th, and 20th Armies did manage to hold a line approximately 20-miles to the east of the city. This action was the first time the Red Army had managed to check the German Blitzkrieg tactics.

Troop leaders converse standing next to a Horch Cross Country vehicle in a forest during operations in August 1941. Note the unit leader armed with the 9mm MP38/40 machine pistol. This weapon was one of the most effective submachine guns ever produced.

Motorcycle combinations inside a forest belonging to Guderian's Panzergruppe II. Motorcyclists could be found in every unit of an infantry and Panzer division, especially during the early part of the war. They were even incorporated in to the divisional staffs, which included a motorcycle messenger platoon.

Infantry with their horses advance through one of the many parts of marshland that covered western Russian. In order to maintain movement pine logs have been laid across the boggy swamps. A Russian civilian has been pressed into service and can be seen moving supplies.

A group of infantry prepare to move out. A number of the troops wear the Zeltbahn shelter quarter. This served as a rain garment and was painted in a three colour splinter camouflage pattern on both sides. One side was in darker greens and brown and the other in lighter shades.

Grenadiers have hitched a lift onboard a StuG.III during operations on the eastern front in the summer of 1941. During the early phase of the invasion of the Soviet Union the StuG proved its worth, especially clearing out enemy infantry in urbanized areas. However, because of its fixed turret it was limited.

Chapter III
Operation Typhoon

Over the next days and weeks that followed the Soviet Army was overwhelmed by the German onslaught. It now seemed that Hitler's grand strategy had yielded such astonishing results that the Soviet Union would soon be conquered. Emboldened by these victorious gains in mid-September Hitler once again began drawing up his plans for the resumption of operations against Moscow. On 16 September, the panzers were finally halted, and their withdrawal to the Moscow front began in earnest.

The regrouping for the final assault on Moscow was a massive logistical nightmare, as the three Panzergruppen, of Guderian, Hoth and Hoppner, were to be used. Of these Hoth's Panzer force was already in place, while Guderian's had to make the long haul back from the Ukraine, and Hoppner's tanks transferred from the Leningrad front. Within two weeks, Bock's forces were in place and ready for action

During the early hours of 30 September 1941, the first phase of the attack on Moscow began, code-named 'Operation Typhoon'. The assault began with the Panzergruppe II being launched north-eastwards towards Orel, from where it would thrust north behind Yeremenko's Bryansk Front. Two days later on 2 October, the rest of the army group rolled forward with more than 2,000 tanks bearing down on the Soviet capital. Along Bock's entire central front, tanks and infantry poured a storm of fire into the dwindling Red Army ranks. Within hours of the initial attack the Russian front was already crumbling. However, the deeper Bock's forces advanced the heavier the resistance grew. In front of Moscow, the Russians had constructed formidable defences in preparation for the German assault on their capital. Thousands of tanks and artillery were emplaced in the ground up to their gun barrels. Many thousands of mines were laid in the path of the German armoured spearhead. Nearly a million anti-personnel mines and booby traps were set up to kill or maim unsuspecting German infantry. In towns and cities along the road leading to Moscow, the Russians erected thousands of crude defensive barriers.

Although Bock's advance went well, the mass of infantry, consisting of the 2nd, 4th, and 9th Armies, found it difficult to keep pace with the fast moving armour. Consequently, the bulk of them encountered fierce resistance with savagely intense fighting in many areas. To make matters worse, on 6 October the weather began to change as cold, driving rain fell on Army Group Centre. Within hours, the Russian countryside had been turned into a quagmire with roads and field becoming virtually impassable. All the roads leading to Moscow had become boggy swamps. Although tracked vehicles managed to push forward through the mire at a slow pace, trucks and other wheeled vehicles were hopelessly stuck up to their axles in deep boggy mud. Within a month the operation had gone from a rapid drive to a slow crawl. During this period Army Group Centre had lost nearly 35,000 men, excluding the sick and injured, about 240 tanks and heavy artillery pieces, and over 800 vehicles. Surprisingly, the majority of the tanks and other vehicles had not fallen foul of enemy fire, but were lost to the muddy terrain. Supplies were now becoming dangerously low, and fuel and ammunition were hardly adequate to meet the ever-growing demands of the drive to Moscow. With still no prospect of reaching the capital before November concerns began to grow among many of the commanders about the lack of winter supplies.

Despite the mire that reduced virtually the entire central front to a crawl, the weather improved slightly, and six days later on 12 October, 3rd Panzer Army reported it had captured the town of Volokolmask. Following heavy fighting, advanced elements cut the Kalinin Klin highway only 40 miles north of Moscow. The same day further south, tanks from the 4th Panzer Army managed to lunge forward against desperate Russian resistance and smash its way through to Narofominsk. However, some hours later it was halted by blown bridges across the Moscow River. On the southern sector of the front, despite high losses in men and material, Guderian's force bypassed the doomed city of Tula and succeeded in driving north-east, capturing the small towns of Venev and Stalinogorsk. Advanced elements of Bock's central front were now within grasp of Moscow.

Two photographs showing a column of infantry advancing along a road. These soldiers carry the standard infantry equipment including gas mask canister, canteens, mess kit, folding entrenching tools and bread bags. It was quite common, often on long marches, that soldiers frequently attached their helmets either to their belts, or to their Y-straps, as in this photograph.

MG34 machine gunners advance through a field. The leading soldier can be seen clutching an M1924 stick grenade. The vast majority of distances travelled in Russia were done on foot. This was often exhausting for the soldiers, especially when they were compelled to fight before reaching their destination.

A light MG34 machine gun crew rest before resuming their onward journey in Army Group Centre. One of the crew can be seen armed with the MG34 machine gun equipped with the 7.92mm ammunition belt around his neck.

A MG34 heavy machine gun position on the sustained-fire mount. Each infantry battalion contained an MG Company, which fielded eight MG34 heavy machine-guns on the sustained-fire mount.

A vehicle and four motorcycles have halted outside a burning village. By the appearance of the panniers and satchel attached to the motorcycle combinations it is more than likely the vehicles are being used for courier purposes delivering orders, maps, and other important documents to the various units.

A motorcyclist pauses in his march for a drink from his canteen and some of his rations. Motorcyclists could be found in every unit of an infantry and Panzer division, especially during the early part of the war. They were even incorporated in the divisional staffs, which included a motorcycle messenger platoon.

Horse-drawn infantry advance along a road. For 'Operation Typhoon', it was estimated that some 300,000 horses were used for the attack on Moscow, with much of the animals being utilized to tow equipment and ordnance to the front.

A captured Soviet 85mm Model 1939 anti-aircraft gun. This weapon was introduced in early 1940, and although designed primarily as an anti-aircraft gun, like the German 8.8cm, it was widely used in the anti-tank role. The gun was fitted with semi-automatic breech mechanism and a large multi-baffle muzzle brake to reduce recoil and increase the muzzle velocity.

Bicycle troops wait before being signalled into action. One dismounted soldier drinks from his tin mug. Note the ammunition can strapped to the nearest bicycle to resupply his Karabiner 98K bolt action rifle, the standard armament issued to the Wehrmacht during the war.

Assault pioneers flush out a building which has probably been used as a Soviet defensive position. Pioneers were mainly employed as assault troops to supplement the infantry and were employed on the battlefield to attack fortifications and other defensive positions with demolitions and flamethrowers. Here a pioneer is armed with a Flammernwerfer 35.

Pioneers take time out in late September to bath in a river whilst erecting a pontoon bridge across a river: note the towing bridge equipment on a 'T' Type 1 pontoon trailer. Construction of pontoon bridges remained a vital asset, especially to heavy armour, and a well trained Pioneer Bridging Column could build a bridge in a matter of hours.

A German soldier frisks a Soviet POW's pockets for any hidden valuables or weapons. Almost as soon as 'Typhoon' was unleashed in the central sector of the front many thousands of Russian soldiers were encircled, captured or destroyed. However, as the Germans drove deeper into the Soviet heartlands resistance grew and the advance in a number of areas began grinding to a halt with some serious losses in men and equipment.

A 2cm Luftwaffe FlaK gun in action. Note all the spent shells on the ground. As for all the forces on the Eastern Front the Luftwaffe FlaK crews provided combat units and Luftwaffe air defence units with both mobile and fixed anti-tank guns.

A halftrack towing a 15cm heavy field howitzer advances along a road near Orel. Leading the column is an Sdk.fz.251 with a frame antenna. These vehicle are attached to an unidentified unit belonging to Panzergruppe II, which launched its forces north-eastwards towards Orel, from where it would thrust north behind Yeremenko's Bryansk Front.

A Pz.Kpfw.38 (t) tank has halted on a road with other vehicles. Note the national flag draped over the vehicles turret for aerial recognition. This Czech-built tank was relatively successful during operations in the drive on Moscow: however, it was already realized that it was no match against the growing might of the Soviet T-34.

A column of support vehicles pass a destroyed Soviet artillery piece on a road along with other damaged pieces of enemy equipment. On the eastern front support vehicles made a vital contribution to the Army's drive forward, especially when leading units were far ahead of its column.

During the initial stages of 'Typhoon' and Gebirgsjäger artillerymen can be seen next to a 7.5cm Geb36. Spread out across a field, in order to minimize the threat of an aerial attack, are other troops and vehicles.

A 2cm FlaK gun mounted on an Sd.Kfz.10 climbs a steep gradient following another mounted FlaK gun and an Sd.Kfz.251 halftrack. The sides to the vehicles have been folded down for action and one of the crew men can be seen preventing one of the ammunition boxes from sliding off the vehicle. Note the ammunition trailer in tow.

A halftrack towing an 8.8cm FlaK gun wades through a shallow part of a river along with another halftrack and a light four-wheeled vehicle. Even during the initial stages of 'Typhoon' the supply situation was exacerbated by the almost complete lack of proper roads throughout the Soviet Union. Halftracks and other tracked vehicles were utilized to help speed up the supply of ammunition and other equipment desperately required for the front.

A FlaK crew of a 2cm FlaK30 gun mounted on the rear of a camouflaged Sd.Kfz.10/4 on the eastern front. The gun's barrel has been elevated towards the sky, the crew having evidently detected enemy aircraft activity. The hinged sides have been completely removed for combat, to allow the crew plenty of space for manoeuvre.

A rifle company crosses an open field in a well-dispersed formation. These troops often moved in file formation and could rapidly be deployed into line at a moment's notice. The file was regarded as the easiest and most effective way to control a rifle company during an advance and it allowed them not only to gain significant ground but without losing momentum either.

A PaK crew with their 3.7cm PaK35/36. A typical infantry regiment was comprised of three infantry battalions, an infantry gun company with six 7.5cm l.IG18 and two 15cm s.IG33 guns, and an anti-tank company with twelve 3.7cm PaK35/36 guns.

Infantry march along a road churning up dust as they push forward east of Orel in early October 1941. These troops belong to the 134th Infantry Division, which was part of XXXIV Army Corps under the command of General Metz.

A crew of a Pz.Kpfw.III halt during their drive on the Soviet capital in order to refuel. The vast distances in which the Panzerwaffe had to travel was immense and supply lines were constantly being overstretched, especially by advanced units spearheading far in front of the advancing column.

A Pz.Kpfw.III advances at speed along a dusty road during its long drive on Moscow. Each panzer division was fully equipped when it invaded Russia. Each division fielded two motorized infantry regiments with two infantry battalions.

Three StuG.III's advance along a road passing a halted column of vehicles. During Barbarossa the StuG.III was detailed to the infantry divisions that fought at focal points in the battle. The StuG.III performed extremely well in an infantry support role. But as the war progressed and the Soviets began introducing heavier armour, the hard pressed StuG.III was constantly called upon by the infantry for offensive and defensive fire support.

Horch Cross Country vehicles cross a heavy pontoon bridge bound for the front during Army Group Centre's drive on Moscow in early October 1941.

A Junker 52 (Ju-52) transport aircraft takes off from a temporary landing strip. Whilst the Ju-52 replenished much needed supplies and troops to the front and airlifted wounded personnel, the aircraft was slow and very lightly armed against fighters. As a result, it suffered terrible losses in almost all actions on the Eastern Front. Many types of replacement were built, but none was as popular or reliable as the Ju-52.

Troops trying to move a vehicle along a muddy road. These vehicles belong to the 4th Panzer Division. It was on 3 October 1941, that the 4th Panzer Division arrived at Orel, following successful attacks from the town of Kromy. This had been a battle of attrition, with serious losses in men and equipment.

Two photographs showing what is probably a forward artillery observation post with an observer estimating the range to a target using a 6x30 Sf 14Z Scherenfernrohr (scissor binoculars). Observation posts were normally located well forward of the infantry they supported, and it was essential that they were well dug-in and well concealed if they were to remain undetected. The Germans nicknamed these as 'Donkey's Ears'.

Infantry cross a pontoon bridge. It shows an excellent display of an infantryman's combat equipment. A web battle pack carrier is attached to his support straps to which his mess kit and shelter quarters are fastened. Many of the men wear their M1938 field cap and have their M1935 steel helmet attached to their kit.

A halftrack tows a medical vehicle along a muddy road. The halftrack was undoubtedly the workhorse of the Eastern Front, especially along the terrible road system that plagued seemingly endless miles of terrain. Its effective towing capability ensured that troops and ordnance often got through unhindered.

Vehicles belonging to the 20th Panzer Division advancing along a muddy road. For the Panzer divisions in Army Group Centre, mud was a formidable foe. The mud produced from a few hours of rain was enough to turn a relatively typical uneven Russian road into a quagmire.

Infantry standing next to a muddy road during the long march to Moscow. The Soviet Union proved to be a completely alien environment to the German soldier, and the distances travelled soon proved more of problem than ever imagined. Russia would not only test the endurance of the German soldier's physical stamina, but also his weapons and supplies.

A horse-drawn cart pressed into service by the Landser has halted in the mud. One of the soldiers tends to his wounded comrade lying inside the cart. Many horse-drawn wagons such as this were requisitioned by the Wehrmacht to transport a variety of supplies and injured or even dead soldiers.

Infantrymen struggle to free vehicles stuck in the mire along a road during Army Group Centre's drive towards the Soviet capital. Often many man-hours were wasted trying to haul stranded vehicles or artillery pieces through the mud. The terrible road system had seriously delayed the German advance, and the Russian winter was now fast approaching.

Support vehicles belonging to Guderian's Panzergruppe II negotiate a muddy road. Due to the appalling road conditions the use of the main roads was restricted generally to priority class vehicles such as tanks and halftracks. Next in priority came the ammunition columns and fuel convoys, and then the reinforcements needed to nourish the advance. The nearer to the battle zones, the worse the road system became.

A vehicle struggles through the mud on a typical Russian road in the Orel sector of the front during the drive on Moscow in October 1941. In western Russian the all-weather roads had not been constructed to carry the amount and weight of traffic that now used them and the surfaces began to break up under the strain creating muddy roads.

Two vehicles struggle through the quagmire during Army Group Centre's drive. The mud produced from a few hours of rain in Russia was enough to immobilize whole columns of wheeled transport, even tanks.

A common scene in central Russia, even during the summer months when there was heavy rain. Here halftracks and a motor vehicle struggle along a road that has been turned into a sea of mud. Even after a short downpour the roads in central Russia could easily be turned into a muddy pool of water, often bringing the advance to a crawl or standstill.

Soldiers advance along a muddy road with supplies being towed by animal draught. All the troops on foot are wearing the Zeltbahn shelter quarter in order to protect themselves from the heavy rain. There were various methods of wearing the Zeltbahn. It could be used as a poncho for dismounted troops, as in this photograph, and it could also be worn for mounted and bicycle mounted soldiers.

An interesting photograph showing horses attempting to free a vehicle that has become stuck in the mire. The Landser relied heavily on animal draught for motive power. Although the infantry regiments were supplied with light trucks to move ordnance and other equipment to the front, many infantry regiments, especially the recently raised divisions, relied heavily on horses. Motorized prime movers were preferred as it was necessary to rapidly move weapons and supplies from position to position in order to survive and effectively engage the enemy.

Army Group Centre in October 1941, facing the horrors of mud in the Orel sector. In western Russia the all-weather roads had not been constructed to carry vast amounts of heavy traffic. This road is on the Roslavl highway and has been reduced to a mud track nearly one metre deep.

Destroyed Soviet artillery on a road is a grim reminder of how powerful the German drive was on its advance to Moscow. Along Bock's entire central front, panzer and infantry units poured a storm of fire into the dwindling Red Army ranks. Within hours of the initial attack the Russian front was already collapsing.

Outside a village the Wehrmacht display some captured battlefield booty including the Soviet Maxim 1910 machine gun. The M1910 was mounted on a cumbersome wheeled mount with a gun shield; however, two years later in 1943 it was replaced by the SG-43 Goryunov.

A very long column of horse drawn transport pushes forward during Operation Typhoon. Most motive power within the regiments of the infantry divisions came from draught animals. An average artillery regiment had an establishment of some 2,500 troops and 2,274 horses. The latter of which drew over 200 wagons and artillery caissons.

Infantrymen seen with piles of Soviet battlefield booty. Some of the captured gear consist of the Maxim 1910 machine gun, the SVT40 automatic rifle and the 7.62mm self-loading rifle. A German PaK35/36 antitank gun sits nearby. Behind the weapon a large contingent of Soviet POWs can be seen seen under guard.

The crew of a 15cm s.FH18 howitzer pose for the camera next to their weapon, which is concealed beneath camouflaged netting. By the angle of the gun barrel the weapon appears to have been directed against a ground target. The white armbands on two crewmembers probably suggest that the operation is under simulated conditions and the artillerymen are in training.

Infantrymen belonging to the 260th Infantry Division halt on the edge of a village during their drive on Moscow in October 1941. A typical German infantry division consisted of three infantry regiments, an artillery regiment, reconnaissance, anti-tank, pioneer, and signal battalions, plus divisional services. Trucks transported much of the supporting battalions, but there were many infantry that marched on foot including all the supply columns that were horse-drawn.

A typical scene on the eastern front in Army Group Centre. A horse drawn cart carrying supplies has become stuck in the mud and a soldier is trying to relieve its rear wheels from the mud. German commanders observed with considerable alarm how roads simply vanished in just a few hours of rain, and soon realized how dependent they were on the few all weather roads that had been built in Western Russia.

Chapter IV
Winter Warfare

While Army Group Centre was making its final preparations for an all-out assault against Moscow, General Erich von Manstein prepared to assault the Crimea with his 11th Army. When he took command of 11th Army in September 1941, he had been assigned two divergent missions: to overrun the Crimea and to take Rostov.

On 24 September 1941, Manstein attacked south into the Perekopisthmus with General Erik Hansen's LIV Corps. General Kuebler's XLIX Gebirgsjäger-Corps was put in reserve, ready at a moment's notice to exploit any breakthrough and drive on Sevastopol, the great Soviet naval fortress on the southwestern tip of the peninsula. Manstein was to drive through the Crimea to Sevastopol but all he had to defend his eastern flank was General Hans von Salmuth's 30th Corps and six unreliable Romanian brigades.

On 28 September Hansen's LIV Corps attacked towards the Perekopisthmus against six Soviet divisions and fought a bitter action there. Although Hansen's Corps incurred heavy casualties, it managed to capture 10,000 prisoners, 112 tanks, and 135 guns in the process. But the victory could not be exploited, because the Soviets attacked Manstein's eastern flank. Whilst 30th Corps held its ground under merciless enemy fire, the Romanians collapsed, and Manstein had to rush Kuebler's Korps to the Nogav Steppe.

It seemed that the Red Army had temporarily halted the German drive through the Crimea, but it had exposed its right flank to an attack by Kleist's 1st Panzer Army to the north. Between 5 – 10 October both Kleist and Manstein co-operated in a battle of encirclement on the Sea of Azov. In the process they managed to destroy the 18th Army. The Germans, however, once again incurred heavy casualties and gave the Russians three weeks to reinforce Sevastopol and the Crimea.

The defence of Sevastopol was provided mainly by the Black Sea Fleet and the separate Coastal Army under Petrov. The city garrison had one brigade, three regiments and 19 battalions of marine corps. Scattered around Sevastopol was a string of defensive positions consisting of 82 pillboxes with naval guns, 220 machine-gun earth-and-timber emplacements and various other bunkers, 20 miles of tank ditches, 30 miles of wire entanglements, and 9,600 mines were laid to improve the defence.

On 30 October 1941, a rapid German thrust was launched against Sevastopol. German forces took the Balaklava Hills, and then pushed at breakneck speed through into the city of Sevastopol from the north, north-east and east, but were beaten back. The Germans then encircled the city. During this time the city was reinforced by the sea, receiving the bulk of Russian troops evacuated from Odessa.

For the next few days German forces began bringing up additional artillery in an effort to soften enemy defensive positions before they attacked the fortress of Sevastopol. On 11 November 60,000 Axis soldiers launched another attack, but after ten days of bitter fighting were forced to halt the attack primarily because Manstein decided to attack the enclave's southern flank. Whilst the southern part of Sevastopol was not as heavily defended the terrain in the region was difficult, and Manstein failed to force a breakthrough. On 4 December the local Soviet command reported that the defences had been reestablished.

With the defences reestablished, von Manstein abandoned the attack in the south and transferred his forces to the north. The Germans also moved in their largest artillery piece, the 80cm gun, Schwerer Gustav, in preparation for another attack. For the next five days the Germans unleashed a massive artillery barrage on the city.

On 17 December 1941, six German infantry divisions and two Romanian brigades with 1,275 guns and mortars, over 150 tanks and 300 aircraft launched the second attack. The Luftwaffe too was used, but due to severe weather conditions, operations were limited, meaning that the Russians could further reinforce the enclave.

Whilst Manstein's force had been battling towards Sevastopol, in other areas of the southern front Army Group South was continuing its relentless drive East and trying its best to secure the Donetz river line and Rostov before winter set in. Since the summer the 6th Army had been spearheading its forces with considerable success in the area. Yet much of the 6th Army was not mechanized. There were some 25,000 horses alone that were used to move guns and supplies. Although this type of transportation did not cause its commanders initial concern, by the time the army arrived at the upper Donets River in October 1941 the weather began to change. Cold driving rain fell on the Army Group's front and within hours the Russian countryside had been turned into a quagmire, with roads and fields becoming virtually impassable. Many of the roads leading to the Caucasus via the city of Rostov had become boggy swamps. Although tanks and other tracked vehicles managed to push through the mire at slow pace, draft animals, trucks and other wheeled vehicles became hopelessly stuck in deep boggy mud. To make matters worse, during November the German supply lines became increasingly overstretched, their vehicles were breaking down, and casualty returns were mounting. Stiff resistance too began to hinder progress. As the situation deteriorated further Rundstedt, against Hitler's

Two photographs showing a 15cm artillery crew poised for action in the snow in early November 1941. The artillery piece is in an elevated position and is being prepared for action. The power of these heavy field guns could hurl its destructive charge miles into the enemy lines, sometimes with devastating results.

Two photographs showing soldiers armed with an MG34 machine gun mounted on a on its tripod mount. The MG34 had tremendous staying power against enemy infantry and during the march on Moscow soldiers took to continuously deploying their machine guns in the most advantageous offensive and defensive positions. These infantrymen are more than likely attached to an artillery battery. Artillery batteries were provided with two 7.92mm light machine-guns for self-defence both from ground and aerial attack.

orders, ordered Kleist's 1st Panzer Army to evacuate Rostov and fall back over the Mius River, some 60 miles west of the city. On the night of 30 November Rundstedt was relieved of his command and replaced by Reichenau. A few days later a forty-three-year-old staff officer called Friedrich Wilhelm Ernst Paulus was promoted to commander of the 6th Army. It was hoped that through Paulus's leadership the winter of 1941 would be mastered. However, not even Paulus's ardent determination could prevent his force, or indeed the entire front of Army Group South, from coming to a standstill across the freezing plains of the Soviet Union.

Elsewhere both Panzer and infantry divisions were experiencing terrible conditions as the temperature along the front lines plummeted. In Army Group Centre, where Bock's forces had been advancing towards Moscow, conditions had deteriorated considerably.

During the last two weeks of October, weather conditions became much worse. Heavy rain, snow showers, and enveloping mists made movement almost impossible for Bock's forces. In front of these exhausted troops stood General Zhukov's men, who were determined to defend Moscow to the last. Even when the Germans managed to break through their lines, the Russian rearguards never left their position until they were literally blown off it. Slowly the movement of the Panzers halted through fatigue, shortages, and the freezing climate. The Soviets then exploited the situation and attacked them without respite, pulverising their positions with their Katyusha rocket mortars.

In early November German supply lines were considerably overstretched, their vehicles were breaking down, and casualty returns were mounting by the hour. Stalling in front of Moscow, Bock stated that he would have to regroup Army Group Centre for the final march on the capital. Yet, several days later on 15 and 16 November, his army group, still exhausted and understrength, was ordered by Hitler to push forward toward Moscow and capture the city before the snow blizzards arrived in December. At first the advance went well and Hoth's Panzergruppe threatened to break open the whole Russian position in the north west. To the south Guderian's force also came close to achieving its objective. But the freezing temperatures had caused well over 50% of frostbite casualties in each of the regiments of the 4th Panzer Division. Slowly the division deteriorated in the snow, and by the end of November was near to collapse. With the almost total destruction of Guderian's force he ordered his men to fight a defensive battle of attrition in the terrible arctic conditions.

In spite of the terrible state of Army Group Centre Hitler ordered that Bock should continue with its drive on Moscow regardless of the terrible shortages in men and material. Day by day, the seeds of disaster grew. By early December, the situation became much worse as the temperature dropped. Many soldiers were now reluctant to emerge from their shelter during the blizzards to fight. Hundreds of tanks were abandoned in the drifting snow. By mid-December, with the situation worse than ever, the temperatures reached 40 degrees below zero. Despair gripped Heeresgruppe Mitte. On Christmas Eve, Guderian had less than 40 Panzers in his entire command; Hoeppner had only one unit of more than 15 tanks, and still they were told not to withdraw.

Hitler's policy to hold his battered frost bitten forces in front of Moscow had in fact saved ground, but at an alarming expenditure in men and material. The Russians, as predicted, finally ran out of power because of the harsh weather, and were unable to achieve any deep penetration into the German lines. This had consequently saved Army Group Centre from complete destruction. Although Hitler was later to say that the battle for Moscow was his finest hour, his army had in fact failed to capture the city, being crucified by the Russian winter and by fanatical Soviet resistance. But much of the failure of Operation Typhoon was essentially due to the remarkable Russian recovery and their winter offensive. The battle had completely altered the Wehrmacht from its glorious days in June and July 1941. From now on, it was to carry the scars of Operation Typhoon to its grave.

A light MG34 machine gun crew pause during their march in the snow. It is evident in this photograph how unprepared these troops were for winter combat. The majority of them wear their standard army issue greatcoat. Two of the men are seen wearing the woolen toque, which was a popular winter item during this period of the war. Scarves were sometimes worn with the toque in order to help provide the wearer with additional insulation.

Two signalmen with two small field telephone cable reel. This type of reel could be drawn by hand, as in this photograph, or behind a bicycle. Often the cables were connected on poles to a radio truck (Funkkraftwagen). However for speed on the battlefield signalmen frequently laid them on the round, but the cables were susceptible to damage from passing traffic running over them.

Two Panzer crewmen pose for the camera standing in front of their Pz.Kpfw.IV. The Pz.Kpfw.IV became the most popular Panzer in the Panzerwaffe and remained in production throughout the war. Originally the Pz.Kpfw.IV was designed as an infantry support tank, but soon proved to be so diverse and effective that it earned a unique offensive and defensive role on the battlefield.

A halftrack towing a trailer full of supplies including a motorcycle advances along a road in the snow during operations in the early winter of 1941. These troops are probably pioneers attached to a bridge building column unit.

A light MG34 machine gunner with his No2 taking-up a position in the snow. The soldiers wears the standard army issue greatcoat with a woolen toque beneath their M1935 steel helmet.

Infantrymen rest during their long foot march and tuck into some of their rations before resuming their advance. All the men wear the standard issue M1938 field cap and standard equipment worn by the Landser during this period of the war.

Three photographs show whitewashed 21cm Mrs18 guns being readied for action by their crew. This heavy mortar large-calibre gun had a range of almost 17 km, the large calibre and its enormously effective fire making the mortar a very effective artillery weapon. Although it was hindered by its weight of some 16.7 tons it remained in service until the end of the war. It was widely used for destroying enemy fortifications and well dug-in positions.

A PaK crew with their 7.5cm l.IG18 gun man-handling their gun to another position. This weapon was one of the first post World War One guns to be issued to the Wehrmacht and later the Waffen-SS. The gun was light and robust and employed a shotgun breech action.

A soldier struggles through the snow with his horse towing a sled. Using a sled was one of the most effective means of moving infantry equipment from one part of the battlefront to another. During 'Operation Typhoon', in spite of the terrible arctic conditions, the German Army relied heavily on the horse for motive power. Sometimes thousands were lost each day due to combat or extreme weather conditions.

A 2cm FlaK gun partially covered by white sheeting in order to help conceal it in the snow. Once this gun was leveled by three adjustable feet, the gun layer would then climb into the seat and the gun would be ready for action.

Troops in a defensive position in the snow. As with virtually all soldiers during 'Operation Typhoon' the men are inadequately clothed for cold weather, in spite of wearing their greatcoats. In order to compensate for their armies inadequacies they wear captured Russian ushanka fur caps instead of the standard issue M1938 field cap.

Troops are seen constructing a shelter from the snow. Under extreme arctic conditions, it was vital to bring every man under cover at night, and guard duty was limited to short periods. The igloos the men built had a number of advantages – being made of snow, they were camouflaged, and their thick walls were wind-proof and provided insulation against the cold.

A sentry on guard duty. This soldier wears the standard infantryman's greatcoat, which was a long double-breasted item of clothing and when properly worn was designed to reach the wearers calf. The greatcoat was made of high quality woollen content cloth. Sometimes the lining of the garment was made with an extra thick blanket lining in order to increase protection against the cold. The colour of the greatcoat was a greenish shade of field-grey. It had a deep dark blue-green collar and two rows of six field-grey metal buttons. It had two slanted hip pockets, both of which had rounded pocket flaps. The army enlisted mans leather belt was normally worn with this pre-war item of clothing where ammunition pouches and other items of personal equipment could be attached. His M1935 steel helmet has received an application of winter whitewash paint.

Soldiers pose for the camera. A light MG34 machine can be seen on its bipod with a 250 round ammunition box. Note the squad leader with the usual NCOs equipment being worn such as the MP39/40 magazine pouches and a pair of 6x30 field binoculars.

Troops protect themselves against the bitter night ahead using Zeltbahn shelter quarter as protection. Over the coming weeks soldiers in a number of sectors of the front were compelled to fight against stiffening enemy attacks that were designed not only to hold back the enemy but to deny them any shelter.

An NCO scours the terrain looking through a pair of 6x30 field binoculars. He wears the M1935 greatcoat, which was the most common winter garment issued in the first Russian winter campaign. He wears grey woollen mittens, black woollen toque and M1935 grey steel helmet. His main armament is the P38 in its hard tortoise shell casing. Attached to his black leather infantryman's belt are two M1924 stick grenades.

An MG34 machine gunner in a defensive position in the snow. In order to help blend in with the local terrain he wears a piece of crude white sheeting. By November 1941 large batches of winter garments were hastily dispatched to the front line combat troops comprising of a number of different styles of white, lightweight covers. There were snow shirts, two-piece snow suits, snow overalls, and the single-piece snow overall. As the bitter temperatures dropped during late November and early December further attempts by the troops to improvise on their winter wear increased including the use of animal skin coats and captured Russian stocks of clothes, which were often lined with fur.

Opposite: Waffen-SS troops pause during their march. By October 1941 the Germans strove desperately to develop and dispatch items of clothing that would not only help camouflage their troops in the snow, but would help protect them against the cold climate as well. It was therefore found necessary to supply the front line combat troops with a thin white cotton cover, cape or suit that could be worn over all uniforms and equipment and could easily be washed and cleaned.

Infantrymen queue with their canteens for food from a supply truck. By November supplies were now becoming dangerously low, and food, fuel and ammunition were hardly adequate to meet the ever-growing demands of the drive to Moscow.

A squad leader armed with a MP38/40 submachine gun leads his men forward through the snow. He wears an animal fur skin coat and Russian ushanka fur cap. His machine gun was used extensively by paratroopers, tank crews, platoon and squad leaders, and other troops throughout the war. The weapon was characterized by its low rate of fire and low recoil.

Wehrmacht troops stand next to a shelter somewhere on the Ostfront in Army Group Centre. By early November 1941 the day time temperature had dropped to 25 degrees below zero. In a number of areas along the front the freezing conditions caused the attacks to stall. Troops were therefore compelled to build shelters in order to stay alive.

A group of troops poses for the camera in front of a makeshift shelter in a forest. Zeltbahn shelter quarters have been utilized to provide the troops not only with shelter from the bitter elements, but for concealment as well. The soldiers appear to be wearing felt insulated boots in order to help keep their feet warm. Although the German leather boot helped combat short-term adverse weather conditions, over a long period of time soldiers found that their boots retained the damp, and constant exposure to the snow and wet often caused them to fall apart. As a result, this allowed the socks to become exposed or wet and caused unprecedented cases of frostbite. To help fight against frozen feet soldiers began lining their boots with straw or paper, but there were little of those two materials available across the vast icy wastelands of the Soviet Union.

A column of Soviet PoWs escorted under armed guard along a track to the rear. Although by November the Germans were suffering along a frozen front, fierce fighting continued to rage. As a result of a number of successful engagements thousands of Russian soldiers were encircled, killed or captured.

Motorcyclists pause during their advance and can be seen with a motorcycle combination. Although the motorcycle was a versatile vehicle and built for speed, in Russia, especially during the winter period, these vehicles performed relatively badly.

Two infantrymen pose for the camera. As with virtually all soldiers during 'Typhoon' the troops were inadequately clothed for cold weather combat, in spite of wearing their greatcoats. In order to compensate for their army's inadequacies they wear Russian ushanka fur caps instead of the standard issue M1938 field cap or M1935 steel helmet, which were regarded as 'freezer boxes' when worn in extreme cold temperatures.

An infantryman wearing the new winter white snow overall over his standard army greatcoat. His M1935 steel helmet has received an application of winter whitewash paint. He is standing inside a trench observing the enemy through a pair of 6x30 field binoculars.

Two soldiers wearing the standard army greatcoat and displaying all the equipment associated with a soldier of this period including the Karbiner 98K bolt action rife and MP38/40 submachine gun. Their M1935 steel helmet has been covered with white canvas sheeting in order to help camouflage them in the snow-covered terrain.

A 12-ton Sd.Kfz.8 towing what appear to be components for the 21cm Mrs.18 has halted on a frozen road. Three of the crew members wearing the army greatcoats stand next to the halftrack.

A soldier wearing the standard army greatcoat and ushanka fur cap riding on a Pz.Kpfw.IV bound for the front lines. At first virtually all of the German vehicles fighting on the Eastern Front did not receive any type of winter whitewash paint and retained their original dark grey camouflage scheme, making them more susceptible to attack in the snow.

Troops in the process of camouflaging a Horch Cross country vehicle from both ground and aerial observation. Wood is also being applied to build a structure around the vehicle in order to conceal it better and to keep the vehicle's components from freezing in the arctic conditions.

Opposite: Soldiers preparing to move out with a sled containing oak barrels towed by animal draught. Life in the line for these soldiers was a continuous grind. There was little respite – if the Red Army let up for a brief period, the sub-zero temperatures certainly did not.

A Pz.Kpfw.III in the snow fully laden with supplies stowed on the engine deck with a group of Gebirgsjäger troops. Three of the soldiers wear the white camouflage cover fitted over their Bergmütze.

The march through Russia, especially during the winter period, was exhausting for the troops. Here in this photograph a soldier sleeps on a makeshift bed. Sheeting and a pillow have been placed on a piece of boarding resting on a bush in order to avoid any contact with the snow. Behind him is a HF 12 small kitchen wagon.

Two soldiers, one a squad leader armed with a MP38/40 submachine gun, pose for the camera in front of a whitewashed support vehicle. Note the snow chains secured to the rear wheels of the truck providing better traction across the snow.

A support truck leading a column of vehicles moves along a frozen road passing an infantryman. The lorry displays the letter 'G' indicating Guderian's Panzergruppe II. By this stage of the invasion Guderian's troops had been seriously curtailed by the harsh weather conditions. High losses in men and equipment had severely hampered operations.

A 15cm s.FH18 heavy field howitzer being readied for action. Out in the snow the crew have used branches to try and conceal the gun as much as possible. This type of camouflaging was undertaken not just to hide the weapon but served to deny the enemy the ability to identify what type of artillery piece occupied the position.

A typical scene before Moscow in December 1941, showing a column of troops trudging towards the front. All across the front hundreds of tanks and armoured vehicles had become mired, and as a result the majority were simply abandoned in the drifting snow. By mid-December, with the situation worse than ever, the temperatures reached 40 degrees below zero. Despair gripped Army Group Centre.

A group of soldiers pose for the camera in a light MG34 machine gun position. A number of Karabiner 98K bolt action rifles can also be seen. All the troops wear the standard army issue great coat and have used a variety of methods to camouflage their M1935 steel helmet.

A variety of vehicles from Guderian's Panzergruppe II spread out across a vast open frozen field. As Guderian's force advanced nearer to the Soviet capital the Russians became more determined than ever to stem the German onslaught by any means possible, from blowing bridges, laying endless anti-tank traps, mining and destroying main roads.

MG34 troops, one dressed in an animal fur coat, and the other in the standard army greatcoat, pose for the camera beside a knocked out Soviet T-34 tank. Note their MG34 machine gun mounted on a Dreifuss 34 anti-aircraft tripod mount positioned next to the bridge.

A pioneer bridging column unit comprising of motor vehicles and pontoons have crossed a small river. The truck and halftrack are towing bridge equipment 'T' Type 1 pontoon trailers.

Two infantrymen armed with the standard Karabiner 98K bolt action rile, the standard armament issued to the Wehrmacht during the war. The soldiers are totally exposed to the elements and the bitter cold can only well be imagined. The lack of proper clothing is self-evident.

Support vehicles move forward through a forested area. In order to prevent heavy traffic from sinking into the mud pioneers have laid a network of pine logs. This type of construction was widely used by the Germans throughout the war.

A halftrack moving through the thick snow towing a Pz.Kpfw.38 (t) that has probably developed a mechanical problem. All across the front both troops and tanks had ground to a halt in the arctic conditions. The extreme winter of late 1941 had caused the German Army serious delays. As a result the advance stalled along much of the front until the spring thaw of 1942, delaying the conquest of Russia by months. 'Barbarossa' had been a success in terms of the vast distances in which the Wehrmacht had travelled, but coupled with growing enemy resistance and the Russian winter, it had failed to achieve its objective.

German Order of Battle 'Barbarossa' 22 June 1941

Army Group North: Field Marshal Ritter von Leeb

Reserves:

XXIII Army Corps
General Schubert
206th Infantry Division
251st Infantry Division
254th Infantry Division
Gen von Roques
207th Security Division
281st Security Division
285th Security Division
3rd Security Regiment. (mot.) +
619th Guard Battalion (bicycle)
620th Guard Battalion (bicycle)
Higher Police Commander 'North'
Police Regiment 'North'
53rd Reserve Police Battalion (mot)
319th Police Battalion (motorcycle)
321st Police Battalion (motorcycle)

18th Army: General von Kuechler

Reserves

Luftwaffe Flak-Regiment 164
Flak-Battalion II./36, I./51, I./111
272nd Flak Artillery Battalion
604th Army Flak Battalion
563rd Panzerjäger Unit (mot.)
291st Infantry Division
10th MG Battalion (mot.)
403rd Infantry Battalion (bicycle)

531st Coastal Artillery Unit
910th Coastal Artillery Unit

XXXVIII Corps: General von Chappuis

28th Infantry Division

I Corps: General von Both

110th Artillery Regiment (mot.)
609th Artillery Regiment (mot.)
604th FlaK Battalion
185th StuG Unit
11th Infantry Division
1st Infantry Division
21st Infantry Division

XXVI Corps: General Wodrig

818th Artillery Regiment (mot.)
563rd Panzerjäger Unit
402nd Infantry Battalion (bicycle)
61st Infantry Division
217th Infantry Division

Panzergruppe IV: General Hoeppner

16th Army: General Busch

785th Artillery Regiment (mot.)
30th Infantry Division
126th Infantry Division

XXVIII Corps: General Wiktorin

610th Artillery-Regiment (mot.)

665th StuG Battery
667th StuG Battery
122nd Infantry Division
123rd Infantry Division

Army Group Centre: Field Marshal von Bock

9th Army: General Strauss

XXXXII Corps: General Kuntze
87th Infantry Division
102nd Infantry Division
129th Infantry Division
1st SS Mot Infantry Division
106th Infantry Division
110th Infantry Division

Panzergruppe III: General Hoth

XXXIX Corps (mot.): General Schmidt
69th Artillery Regiment (mot.)
Luftwaffe Flak Unit. I./36
605th FlaK Battalion
643rd Panzerjäger Unit
7th Panze Division
Luftwaffe Flak Unit. 84
20th Panzer Division
Luftwaffe Flak Unit. 74
14th Motorized Infantry Division
20th Motorized Infantry Division

LVII Corps (mot.): General Kuntzen
Luftwaffe Flak Unit. I./29
12th Panzer Division
Luftwaffe Flak Unit. 75
19th Panzer Division
Luftwaffe Flak Unit. 85
18th Motorized Infantry Division

4th Army: Field Marshal von Kluge

VII Corps: General Fahrenbacher
41th Artillery Regt. (mot.)
203rd StuG Unit
529th Panzerjäger Unit
7th Infantry Division
23rd Infantry Division
258th Infantry Division
268th Infantry Division
221st Security Division

IX Corps: General Geyer
622nd Artillery Regiment (mot.)
226th StuG Unit
137th Infantry Division
263rd Infantry Division
292nd Infantry Division

XIII Corps: General Felber
17th Infantry Division
78th Infantry Division

XXXXIII Corps: General Heinrici
697th Artillery Regiment (mot.)
786th Artillery Regiment (mot.)
611th FlaK Battalion
131st Infantry Division
134th Infantry Division
252nd Infantry Division

Panzergruppe II: General Guderian

Luftwaffe FlaK Corps I: General von Axthelm
Luftwaffe Flak Regiment 101
Luftwaffe Flak Regiment 104
Luftwaffe Flak Battalion's 77 & 91
Luftwaffe Flak Battalion's I./12, I./22, I./11, II./11

XII Corps: General Schroth
617th Artillery Regiment (mot.)
788th Artillery Regiment (mot.)

279th Flak Artillery Battalion
610th FlaK Battalion
192nd StuG Unit
201st StuG Unit
654th Panzerjäger Battalion (mot.)
Pioneer Regiment (mot.) 507
31st Infantry Division
34th Infantry Division
45th Infantry Division

XXIV Corps (mot.): General von Schweppenburg
623rd Artillery Regiment (mot.)
'Lehr' (mot.)
521st Panzerjäger. (Sfl.)
Pioneer Regiment (mot.) 515
3rd Panzer Division
4th Panzer Division
10th Motorized Infantry Division
1st Cavalry Division
267th Infantry Division

XXXXVI Corps (mot.): General von Vietinghoff
Pioneer Regiment 513
10th Panzer Division.
2nd SS Mot Infantry Division 'Reich'

XXXXVII Corps (mot.): General Lemelsen
792 Artillery Regiment. (mot.)
611th Panzerjäger Battalion
100th Flammpanzer Battalion.
Pioneer Regiment (mot) 413
17th Panzer Division
18th Panzer Division
29th Motorized Infantry Division
167th Infantry Division

Army Group South
Gerd von Rundstedt

11th Army: General Ritter von Schobert

XI Corps: General von Kortzfleisch
76th Infantry Division
239th Infantry Division

XXX Corps: General von Salmuth
198th Infantry Division

LIV Corps: General Hansen
50th Infantry Division
170th Infantry Division

Reserve:
22th Infantry Division
72th Infantry Division

17th Army: General von Stülpnagel

IV Corps: General von Schwedler
295th Infantry Division
262nd Infantry Division
71st Infantry Division
24th Infantry Division
296th Infantry Division

XXXIX Gebirgsjäger-Corps: General of Infantery Kübler
257th Infantry Division
68th Infantry Division
1st Gebirgsjäger Division

LII Corps: General von Briesen
454th Security Department
444th Security Department
101th Jäger Division

Reserve:
97th Jäger Division
100th Jäger Division

6th Army: Field Marshal von Reichennau

XVII Corps: General of Infantry Kienitz
56th Infantry Division: Major General von Oven
62th Infantry Division: Lieutenant General Keiner

XXXXIV Corps: General Koch
9th Infantry Division: Major General Freiherr von Schleinitz
297th Infantry Division: Lieutenant General Pfeffer

Reserve:
LV Corps: General Vierow
213th Security Department

Panzergruppe I: General von Kleist

III Corps: General Mackensen
14th Panzer Division
44th Infantry Division
298th Infantry Division

XXXIX Corps: General Obstfelder
111th Infantry Division
299th Infantry Division

XXXXVIII Corps: General Kempf
11th Panzer Division
57th Infantry Division
75th Infantry Division

Allied Armies

One Hungarian Army and 3th and 4th Romanian Army

Reserve

16th Infantry Division
25th Infantry Division

16th Panzer Division
9th Panzer Division

13th Panzer Division
5th Infantry Division
46th Infantry Division
52th Infantry Division
60th Infantry Division
73th Infantry Division
79th Infantry Division
86th Infantry Division
93th Infantry Division
94th Infantry Division
95th Infantry Division
98th Infantry Division
106th Infantry Division
110th Infantry Division
112th Infantry Division
113th Infantry Division
125th Infantry Division
132th Infantry Division
183th Infantry Division
197th Infantry Division
260th Infantry Division
294th Infantry Division

Soviet Front Order of Battle 22 June 1941

(Main Russian Forces)

Northern Front (Lieutenant General M.M. Popov)
177 Rifle Division
191 Rifle Division
8 Rifle Brigade

1 Mechanized Corps
1 Tank Division
3 Tank Division
163 Motorized Division

7 Army (Lieutenant General F.D. Gorelenko)
54 Rifle Division
71 Rifle Division
168 Rifle Division
237 Rifle Division

14 Army (Lieutenant General V.A. Frolov)
42 Rifle Corps (Major General R.I. Panin)
104 Rifle Division
122 Rifle Division
14 Rifle Division
52 Rifle Division

23 Army (Major General P.S. Pshennikov)
19 Rifle Corps (Major General M.N. Gerasimov)
115 Rifle Division
142 Rifle Division

50 Rifle Corps (Major General V.I. S'cherbakov)
43 Rifle Division
70 Rifle Division
123 Rifle Division

10 Mechanized Corps (Major General I.G. Lazarev)
21 Tank Division
24 Tank Division
198 Motorized Division
7 Motorcyle Regiment

Northwestern Front (Colonel General F.I. Kuznetsov)
65 Rifle Corps (Headquarters)

5 Airborne Corps (Major General I.S. Bergly)
9 Airborne Brigade
10 Airborne Brigade
201 Airborne Brigade

8 Army (Lieutenant General P.P. Sobennikov)
10 Rifle Corps (Major General I.F. Nikolaev)
10 Rifle Division
48 Rifle Division
90 Rifle Division

11 Rifle Corps (Major General M.S. Shumilov)
11 Rifle Division
125 Rifle Division

12 Mechanized Corps (Major General N.M. Shestopavlov)
23 Tank Division

28 Tank Division
202 Motorized Division
10 Motorcycle Regiment

11 Army (Lieutenant General V.I. Morozov)
23 Rifle Division
126 Rifle Division
128 Rifle Division

16 Rifle Corps (Major General F.S. Ivanov)
5 Rifle Division
33 Rifle Division
188 Rifle Division

29 Rifle Corps (Major General A.G. Samokhin)
179 Rifle Division
181 Rifle Division

3 Mechanized Corps (Major General A.V. Kurkin)
2 Tank Division
5 Tank Division
84 Motorized Division

27 Army (Major General M. E. Berzarin)
16 Rifle Division
67 Rifle Division
3 Rifle Brigade

22 Rifle Corps (Major General M.P. Dukhanov)
180 Rifle Division
183 Rifle Division

24 Rifle Corps (Major General K. Kachalov)
181 Rifle Division
183 Rifle Division

Western Front (Colonel General D.G. Pavlov)

3 Army (Headquarters only)

2 Rifle Corps (Major General A.N. Ermakov)
100 Rifle Division
161 Rifle Division

21 Rifle Corps (Major General V.B. Borisov)
17 Rifle Division
24 Rifle Division
37 Rifle Division

44 Rifle Corps (Major General V.A. Yushkevich)
64 Rifle Division
108 Rifle Division

47 Rifle Corps (Major General S.I. Povetkin)
50 Rifle Division
55 Rifle Division
121 Rifle Division
143 Rifle Division

4 Airborne Corps (Major General A.S. Zhandov)
7 Airborne Brigade
8 Airborne Brigade
214 Airborne Brigade
8 Antitank Brigade

17 Mechanized Corps (36 tanks) (Major General M.P. Petrov)
27 Tank Division
36 Tank Division
209 Motorized Division
22 Motorcycle Regiment

20 Mechanized Corps (93 tanks) (Major

General A.G. Niktin)
26 Tank Division
38 Tank Division
210 Motorized Division
24 Motorcycle Regiment

3 Army (Lieutenant General V.I.Kuznetsov)
4 Rifle Corps
27 Rifle Division
56 Rifle Division
85 Rifle Division

11 Mechanized Corps (Major General D.K. Mostevenko)
29 Tank Division
33 Tank Division
204 Motorized Division
16 Motorcycle Regiment
7 Antitank Brigade

4 Army (Lieutenant General A.A. Korobkov)
28 Rifle Corps (Major General V.S. Popov)
6 Rifle Division
42 Rifle Division
49 Rifle Division
75 Rifle Division

14 Mechanized Corps (Major General S.I. Oborin)
22 Tank Division
30 Tank Division
205 Motorized Division
20 Motorcycle Regiment

10 Army (Major General K.D. Golubev)

1 Rifle Corps (Major General F.D. Rubsev)
2 Rifle Division
8 Rifle Division

5 Rifle Corps (Major General A,V, Gamov)
13 Rifle Division
85 Rifle Division
113 Rifle Division

6 Cavalry Corps (Major General I.S. Nikitin)
6 Cavalry Division
36 Cavalry Division
155 Rifle Division

6 Mechanized Corps (Major General M.G. Khatskilevich)
4 Tank Division
7 Tank Division
29 Mechanized Division
4 Motorcycle Regiment

13 Mechanized Corps (Major General P.N. Akhliustin)
25 Tank Division 31 Tank Division
208 Mechanized Division
18 Motorcycle Regiment

Southwestern Front (Lieutenant General M.P. Kirponos)
5 Antitank Brigade

31 Rifle Corps (Major General A.I. Lopatin)
193 Rifle Division
195 Rifle Division
200 Rifle Division

36 Rifle Corps (Major General P.V. Sisoev)
140 Rifle Division
146 Rifle Division
228 Rifle Division

49 Rifle Corps (Major General I.A. Komilov)
190 Rifle Division
197 Rifle Division

199 Rifle Division

55 Rifle Corps (Major General K.A. Koroteev)
130 Rifle Division
169 Rifle Division
189 Rifle Division

1 Airborne Corps (Major General M.A. Usenko)
1 Airborne Brigade
204 Airborne Brigade
211 Airborne Brigade

19 Mechanized Corps (Major General N.V. Feklenko)
40 Tank Division
43 Tank Division
213 Motorized Division

24 Mechanized Corps (Major General S.M. Kondrusev)
45 Tank Division
49 Tank Division
216 Motorized Division

5 Army (Major General M.I. Potapov)
1 Antitank Brigade

15 Rifle Corps (Colonel I.I. Fedyuninsky)
45 Rifle Division
62 Rifle Division

27 Rifle Corps (Major General P.D. Artemenko)
87 Rifle Division
124 Rifle Division
135 Rifle Division

9 Mechanized Corps (Major General K.K. Rokossovsky)
20 Tank Division
35 Tank Division
131 Motorized Division

22 Mechanized Corps (Major General S.M. Kondrusev)
19 Tank Division
41 Tank Division
215 Motorized Division

6 Army (Lieutenant General I.N. Muzychenko)
3 Antitank Brigade

6 Rifle Corps (Major General I.I. Alekseev)
41 Rifle Division
97 Rifle Division
159 Rifle Division

37 Rifle Corps (Brigadier General S.P. Zibin)
80 Rifle Division
139 Rifle Division
141 Rifle Division

4 Mechanized Corps
8 Tank Division
32 Tank Division
81 Motorized Division

15 Mechanized Corps (Major General I.I. Karpezo)
10 Tank Division
37 Tank Division
212 Motorized Division

5 Cavalry Corps (Major General F.V. Kamkov)
3 Cavalry Division
14 Cavalry Division

12 Army (Major General P.G. Ponedelin)
4 Anti-Tank Brigade

13 Rifle Corps (Major General N.K. Kirillov)
44 Rifle Division
58 Rifle Division
192 Mountain Rifle Division

17 Rifle Corps (Major General I.V. Galanin)
60 Rifle Division
96 Mountain Rifle Division
164 Rifle Division

16 Mechanized Corps (Brigadier General A.D. Sokolov)
15 Tank Division
39 Tank Division
240 Motorized Division

26 Army (Lieutenant General F.Ya. Kostenko)
2 Anti-Tank Brigade

8 Rifle Corps (Major General M.G. Snegov)
99 Rifle Division
173 Rifle Division
72 Mountain Rifle Division

8 Mechanized Corps (Lieutenant General D.I. Ryabyshev)
12 Tank Division
34 Tank Division
7 Motorized Division

9 Separate Army (Lieutenant General Ya. T. Cherevichenko)

14 Rifle Corps (Major General D. G. Egorov)
25 Rifle Division
51 Rifle Division

35 Rifle Corps (Brigadier General I.F. Dashichev)
95 Rifle Division
176 Rifle Division

48 Rifle Corps (Major General R. Ya. Malinovsky)
30 Mountain Rifle Division
74 Rifle Division
150 Rifle Division

2 Mechanized Corps (Lieutenant General Y.V. Novoselsky)
11 Tank Division
16 Tank Division
15 Motorized Division

2 Cavalry Corps (Major General P.A. Belov)
11 Cavalry Division
16 Cavalry Division

18 Mechanized Corps (Major General P.V. Volokh)
44 Tank Division
47 Tank Division
218 Motorized Division